Tunes for French Horn Technic

by
James Ployhar
in collaboration with
Fred Weber

To The Teacher

One of the most effective and enjoyable ways to develop technical dexterity on an instrument is through melodies of a technical nature with scale and rhythm variation based on familiar melodies. TUNES FOR TECHNIC is designed with this in mind. Because tunes, melodies and technical variations are interesting and more enjoyable to practice, most students will work more effectively, and over-all results will be excellent. Some of the melodies and variations in TUNES FOR TECHNIC may be challenging and difficult. In this case work up slowly and accurately, then gradually increase tempo. In general, the book progresses in difficulty and correlates with the method book, "The French Horn Student," Part I, and may be also used in conjunction with any elementary French horn method.

The Belwin "STUDENT INSTRUMENTAL COURSE" - A course for individual and class instruction of LIKE instruments, at three levels, for all band instruments.

> **METHOD**
> **The French Horn Student**
> For individual or
> **French Horn Class**
> **Instruction**
> (cannot be used with other brass instruments.)

> **STUDIES AND MELODIOUS ETUDES**
> Supplementary scales, warm-up and technical drills, musicianship studies and melody-like studies.

> **TUNES FOR TECHNIC**
> Technical type melodies, variations, and "famous passages" from musical literature — for the development of technical dexterity.

> **THE FRENCH HORN SOLOIST**
> Interesting and playable graded easy solo arrangements of famous and well-liked melodies.
> Easy piano accompaniments.

Contents

B.I.C.153

Go Tell Aunt Rhody

TRADITIONAL

Crusaders' Hymn

The Garden Dance

FLEMISH FOLK SONG

Looby Lou

Peasant Dance

RUSSIAN FOLK SONG

Drink To Me Only With Thine Eyes

ENGLISH AIR

Faith Of Our Fathers

HEMY

I Love You Truly

Red River Valley

Roses From The South

JOHANN STRAUSS

Carnival Of Venice

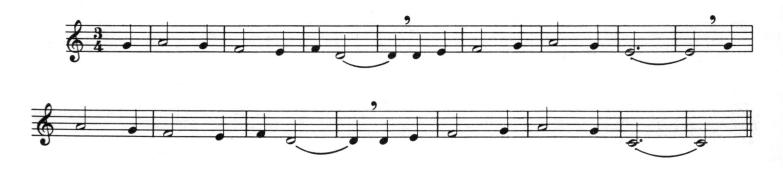

A-Tisket A-Tasket

Sidewalks Of New York

Come To The Sea

The Band Played On

WARD

High School Cadets March

SOUSA

Down In The Valley

TRADITIONAL

Bicycle Built For Two

DACRE

Waltz Melody

NAGELI

March

TRADITIONAL

B.I.C.153

Joyce's 71st Regiment

BOYER

Give My Regards To Broadway

COHAN

Home Sweet Home

BISHOP

Yankee Doodle Boy

Hungarian Dance Theme

You're A Grand Old Flag

B.I.C.153

The Erie Canal

WORK SONG

Night Herding Song

COWBOY SONG

Laura Lee

FOSTER

Sanctus

SCHUBERT

We Wish You A Merry Christmas

When Love Is Kind

Flow Gently, Sweet Afton

The Ash Grove

WELSH AIR

John Peel

ENGLISH HUNTING SONG

Sharpshooters March

Up On The Housetop

HANBY

Can Can

El Relicario

Melody In F

March Slav

TSCHAIKOWSKY

Russian Melody

Trepak Dance

Loch Lomond

SCOTCH AIR

There's Music In The Air

ROOT

Tambourin

RAMEAU

Hymn Tune

GERMAN

The Violins Play

PAGANINI

Country Dance

ENGLISH FOLK SONG

Variations On A Famous Theme

Play slowly at first, then try for speed.

MOZART

Melody

Variation I

Variation II

Variation III-Key of F

B.I.C.153

Theme From Academic Festival

BRAHMS

A - Roving

TRADITIONAL

Camptown Races

FOSTER

Father Of Victory

GANNE

Hymn Of Thanksgiving

In The Gloaming

Andante

HARRISON

mf

'A Frangesa

COSTA

f

Cradle Song

Slowly

BRAHMS

p

Hark! The Herald Angels Sing

MENDELSSOHN

Adeste Fideles

On Our Way Rejoicing

HAYDN

B.I.C.153

Onward Christian Soldiers

SULLIVAN

Home On The Range

TRADITIONAL

Holy, Holy, Holy

DYKES

Deck The Halls

Moderato

WELSH AIR

Carnival In Cremona

Moderato

ITALIAN FOLK SONG

Polka

B.I.C.153

Sweet And Low

Merry Widow

Melody

Andante

SCHUMANN

Barcarolle

Moderato

OFFENBACH

B.I.C.153

Reuben Reuben

Work out all melodies on this page carefully, and then try for speed with accuracy.

Variation

Jingle Bells

Variation

Stately March

Work out all melodies on this page carefully, and then try for speed with accuracy.

Moderato

GERMAN FOLK SONG

Moment Musical

SCHUBERT

The Thunderer March

SOUSA

B.I.C.153

Listen To The Mocking Bird

Work out all melodies in this page carefully, and then try for speed with accuracy.

HAWTHORNE

Melody From The Opera Carmen

BIZET

Musette

BACH

Huntsmens Chorus

VON WEBER